Black and White Coloring Book

© 2010 Richard A. Jones

All rights reserved. Printed in the U.S.A. No part of this publication may be reproduced or transmitted in any form or by any means, electronic or mechanical, including photocopy, recording or any information storage and retrieval system now known or to be invented, without the permission in writing from the author, except by a reviewer who wishes to quote brief passages in connection with a review written for inclusion in a magazine, newspaper or broadcast.

Published in the United States by
Beckham Publications Group, Inc.

ISBN 9780984199198

Black and White Coloring Book

Richard A. Jones

PUBLICATIONS GROUP, INC.
Silver Spring

for my parents—

Gus and Bertie

CONTENTS

Dot Product 7
Forever 8
Quantum Tunneling 10
Self Reclamation 12
When You Needa Friend... 14
Khayelitsha.. 16
Retired... 18
Da Oversoul—Da Remix... 19
The History & Herstory of the 17th Dimensional
    Manifold Involuted into this Spime Erroneously
    Labeled by Space-Monkeys as the Universe 20
Earl-dee-dip... 22
The Beginning of the Beginning.................................... 23
Tuff Shed™ 25
The Last Question 27
Shannon's Law 29
O Light! 31
Old Man Shopping... 32
My HVR-1 mtDNA Sequence 33
Unbreakable Codes.. 36
The Front Forty... 39
Training... 41
Saturday Yard Sale.. 42
Addiction 44

Nothing But Net	46
There Be Doze	48
Folding the Flag at Arlington National Cemetery	50
Old Man's Sex—A Confessional	52
Non-Randomness	54
Watching tv to Relax	56
The Winter Comes Too Soon	58
U Evah?	61
Space Debris	62
Suicide	64
Oil Painting	65
Exponentiation	68
Like a Ship	69
The Perfect Day	71
Love is Messy	72
Don't Sell Me Anything Else	74
Flowchart	77
Schizoid Rat Man	78
Black and White Coloring Book	80
Fear of Listening to Music	83
Sixty-Fifth Vernal Equinox	85
Nap Time	87
I Am a Word	89
Stella	91
Somehow Obama Didn't Do It For Me	92
Grand Pappy Hippie	94

DOT PRODUCT

$$[I \ I] \cdot \begin{vmatrix} You & You & You \\ You & You & You \end{vmatrix}$$

$$= [I \cdot You] + [I \cdot You] = [We + We]$$
$$= [I \cdot You] + [I \cdot You] = [We + We]$$
$$= [I \cdot You] + [I \cdot You] = [We + We]$$

$$= [Us]$$

$$\begin{vmatrix} i & i & i \\ i & i & i \\ i & i & i \end{vmatrix} \times \begin{vmatrix} u & u & u \\ u & u & u \\ u & u & u \end{vmatrix} = \begin{Vmatrix} we & we & we \\ we & we & we \\ we & we & we \end{Vmatrix}$$

$$\begin{vmatrix} us & 0 & 0 \\ 0 & us & 0 \\ 0 & 0 & us \end{vmatrix} \cdot \begin{vmatrix} them & them & them \\ them & them & them \\ them & them & them \end{vmatrix} = \begin{vmatrix} love & 0 & 0 \\ 0 & love & 0 \\ 0 & 0 & love \end{vmatrix}$$

OR

```
   III  III      IIIIIIII       II   II            UUUU
    II  II        II   II       II   II             UU
        II        II   II       II   II     =       UU
        II        II   II       II   II             UU
        II       IIIIIIII      IIIIIIII            UUUU
```

As in I am made up of you and you are made up of I
"You into me, me into you"
I and I brother

FOREVER

I wonder at the fact that
My love for you can survive my dying   tranquilities
In space   In time glorious   Transfinite
wondrous
Fractally   Mandelbroted   Honeycombed π
Death only   Divides it   Circumscribes it
seals it
By diameters   Amendment less   Always and
                                        FOREVER

```
F O R E V E R
F O R E V E R
F  O  R  E  V  E  R
F   O   R   E   V   E   R
F    O    R    E    V    E    R
F     O     R     E     V     E     R
F      O      R      E      V      E      R
F       O       R       E       V       E       R
F        O        R        E        V        E        R
F         O         R         E         V         E         R
F          O          R          E          V          E          R
F           O           R           E           V           E           R
F            O            R            E            V            E            R
F             O             R             E             V             E             R
F              O              R              E              V              E              R
F               O               R               E               V               E               R
F                O                R                E                V                E                R
```

Dot dot dot
. . . and so on and so on
'Til the spaces between the letters
Radiating to eternity

Become SO great
All will have be unwritten   forgotten   disproved
forgiven   abandoned
But YOU and ME
4 evah and 4 evah

QUANTUM TUNNELING

$$\int_{-\infty}^{\infty} \Psi_n^* \Psi_m \, dy = \int_{-\infty}^{\infty} \frac{e^{-y^2} h_m(y) h_n(y) \, dy}{\sqrt{2^{n+m} n! M! \pi}} = 0$$

—David Bohm

So every day
Erday aiight
I drive by the graveyard
Cemetery's symmetry
Where the sign sez
"Backhoe Operator Wanted"
Which is ah bad sign for
A sixty-fo year ol' black man
Me lookin' at
Tha rectangular parallelepiped
Dirt holes for ta bury
The boxes of mortal
Remains a mystery
To me reading
David Bohm's *Quantum Theory*
Today
An' Emmanuel Levinas' *Totality and Infinity*
Yesdiddy
    Until one quote convinced me
    All evidence to the contrary
    If an atomic particle
    In quantum state zero
    Can quantum tunnel
    Outta the deepest gravitational well

Then I can too
Yes I can
"You know I can can"
    For once in a very
    Long time
    Probabilistically
    Whew!
Someone   Somewhere   Somewhen   Somehow
    Quantum states aligned
    Entombed
    In tune with *Totality and Infinity*
    Quantum tunnels outta the Universe
    No matter how deep
    The backhoe operator
    Digs it

SELF RECLAMATION

Rarely
so rarely
i come to my senses
as if by senses
limpidly
airily
for myself
treelike
every cell
a pointed leaf
& shake my head
boughs of neurons
bending in
disbelief
phototropistic double

such that the wise
avoid it preferring
to hide in cartoon

umbral shadows

paranoiac pretensions
tv childhood remembrances
"I don't want to be happy"
"I want to be sad"
"Sunshine/Sunshine"
Dun na na na nana sunshine
Sunshine Sunshine
So tha cartoon sez
Onna DuMont network tv
Circa 1953 launching milkbottles of light

I don't pee hard
like no young'un
no mo' no mo'

an ol' man

pondering the

the weak stream

mini-max to maxi-minimum
$C_{20}H_{28}N_2O_5 \cdot S \cdot HCL$
Flomax® TT

water cannon

micturated

urinated

end to double flushing
triple flushing
"Low-down dirty

heliotropic	On the haters of light	four flusher!"
above my arms	Dying Goethe's plight	To hide the wee wee
limbs	*Young Werther's* night	little lad pee pee
arms	in "Bring me a light!"	obscuring the nighttime
& branches	to see death better	micturate tinkle
Waving	Shuts down the computer	of wee willie winkle
Invitingly	Dark Sadmen struck	dribbling
for the	by milkbottles of light	porcelain side aiming
too tired	x-rayed inside out	Sad sounds
starstruck sparrows	"Want to be happy"	Plinking
to	"Don't want to be sad"	Trying to take a tinkle
light	As I remember	Ol' man taking a piss

WHEN YOU NEEDA FRIEND

    I had a guinea golden
    I lost it in the sand—
    And tho' the sum was simple
    And pounds were in the land—

                  —Emily Dickinson

Sometimes   Ofttimes   Now   Later
    There is nothing
And I think I needa friend   a little friend
Not Like Tony Montana's *lil'fren* in "Scarface"
But like Nietzsche's friend
    A non-existant nothing
Who does not   can not   will not
Be part of the herd
Will to not
Be a sheepeople
    Cliché without
The will to be a soul mate
Cannot exist   being like bubbles filled with smoke
Swirling in the Elysium   forbidden regions of trust
    As ending new beginnings in eternal returns
So like Nietzsche I create one *über freundin*
An imaginary friend
My childhood blanky's comfort
All Zarathustra come striding down
    Unexpected like
From the black forest mountaintop   *Hammer time*

Where the "Cracked brass bells will ring"
Awakening these sheep   You have a friend
Then say nothing   No thing
Will not   can not   does not
      Listen in the revisitation of the nullities
Self-absorbed with
S/HE/IT   Shit's
"I saw the best minds of my generation destroyed by
madness, starving hysterical naked"
      Without a *Light Around the Body*
Carbuncles of syphilitic epileptic   neurasthenic
syncope
Nihilistic nauseam
Thundering herds of Tarantulas
Weaving their *schadenfreude* nets
      Until I thinka I kinda need a
Friend while we await "A rebirth of wonder"
      We are a lonely
Sad
      People

KHAYELITSHA

When I return from the land of exile and silence,
do not bring me flowers.

—Jofre Rocha

Thump-drum Zulu
Cape Town SA
Continents away
Six hours forward shuffle
Six hours back shuffle
Diamonds in the sky
Southern Cross a horizon
Between futures in
Reverse out inside
The townships of
Khayelitsha's shantytowns
One point three
Million bright souls
Lost in the corrugated steel
Weathered gray boards of
Scrap dogs and mal
Nourished indifference
To the obliquely bright
Similes lost in the deductions
Seduced by the simile
As L.W. might say
To Isaiah Shembe
Zulu Messiah whirlwind

Shaka Zulu
As nothing is like to like
Something else for days
As Africa's sunlight is
Rhythmically fractured on
The blinded rich by poor
Skinny AIDS orphans
Squinting at the 'Merican
Negroes peeking shyly at
Their sad trash littered
Truths' in ashy bare feet
In streets where we
Thumping equally primitive
Slim Shady iPod beats
Cross thumbs when
We meet to shake seething souls
Shaky shake
Shaka Shaka
Zuma Zuma
Brothers in our motley veins
In Khayelitsha in Gugulethu
Makes me want to
Shaka Shaka
Gouge out my eyes
For what they see

RETIRED

The day today
We will not waste the light
"Don't help them bury the light"
Roll away the stone
Will not will not
Today as starlight still shines
On the retired (re) tired
Superannuated
Tired yet again
As in re-tired
Washed up
Put out to pasture
Or put out in
A baseball game
Retired in the bottom
Of the ninth
A run behind
5-3 routine play
I am retired
Useless and alone
Feeling tired lord
But never retired
Tired x Tired
Equals Tired^2
Tired to the meta-level
Washed up
"Clean and so clean clean"
Clean with no place to
Go go

DA OVERSOUL—DA REMIX

My thin nightshirt
Insufficient cover for
Olber's blazing sky
Shingled roof not enough
Protection from the Machian abysses
Of night's paradox
No shelter from Infinity in All
Directions rooflessness
A billion billion
Ersatz eerie stars spewing out the ergs
No skin thick enough
To shutter or protect the
Shadow within my soul
The soulful smile
The gigabit scorn
In the eternal silver
Light from which there
Is no surcease
No outside
No inside
An accomplishment
"Death is like a
High fastball out over the plate
Where you can get to it"
"Death is like going to the dentist
& having a rotten tooth extracted
Cuz it's so much better afterwards"
"Death's an adhesion
To be torn away"
An accomplishment

THE HISTORY & HERSTORY OF THE 17TH DIMENSIONAL MANIFOLD INVOLUTED INTO THIS SPIME ERRONEOUSLY LABELED BY SPACE-MONKEYS AS THE UNIVERSE

Googolplex^{Googolplex} $(100^{100})^{100}$ tu da tuda tu da tu da
till ya get da idea tu da
Nothing for eternity
"
"
"

Ditto *ad nauseam*
Until
(More of the same nothing)$^\infty$
And then
More (NOTHING x NOTHING)$^\infty$
"
"
"

Ditto *ad nauseam*$^{-2}$
Then ("Dividing thens by now / is how to hump a cow")
Nothing $\emptyset^\emptyset$ (Nothing to the nothing power)
$\{\emptyset\}^\infty$ (Nothing to the infinity power)

$\prod^\infty$ (multiplying zero an infinite number or times) times $\aleph_0$ times all the power sets of $\aleph_0$ times all the power sets of [$\aleph_0$ times all the power sets of $\aleph_0$]
Followed by sempiternity^{nth}
Then 0/0 (zero divided by zero = ∞)

"
"

Singularity!! (factorial)
Sumpin' from nutin'
Nut rolling across the sky
Sui generis
Duh?
Ex nihilo
T.E. = P.E. + K.E. = $mR^2 [\frac{1}{2} H^2 - \frac{4}{3} \pi \rho]$
Duh?
Du da du Da
Du da du Da Day
Until ta Dah
You!
For what
Huh?

EARL-DEE-DIP

Earl-dee-dip
Earl-dee-dip
Earl-dee-dip earl-dee-dip
Freakin' A righty-right
Earl-dee-dip

La de da
La de day
La lay do dah day
Earl-dee-dip

Earl-dee-dip
Do dah
Do dah
Do dah
Do dah day

Earl-dee-dip
Earl-dee-dip
Earl-dee-dip

Ya freakin' righty-right
Earl-dee-dip

THE BEGINNING OF THE BEGINNING

> Now, this is not the end. It is not even the beginning of the end. It is not even the end of the beginning's end. Nor is it the beginning of the end's beginning. Nor the end's beginning of the ending, beginning with what seemed to have been the end of the beginning, when in actual fact it was the beginning of the beginning's end. But, it may be the beginning of what appeared to be the end of the beginning of the end. That, or the middle.
>
> —Winston S. Churchill

There is nothing of course
Yet no *word* for nothing
'Cause then it would be *something*
Sumpen
No *logos* nothing
For there *is* the beginning
And there is the beginning of the beginning
The beginning of the middle of the beginning
The end of the beginning of the middle of the beginning
The beginning of the end of the beginning
The middle of the end of the end of the middle of the beginning
The end of the beginning
Unexpectedly the beginning of the cliché
The beginning of the beginning of the end

The middle of the beginning of the end
The end of the beginning of the end
Resulting in the end of the beginning
Begun becomes something
Whatever
Somehow
Until it begins again
To look like
Nothing again in the end
A Twirly bird
Googaw
Googly-eyed
Idiot spinning
In the tinkly
Shining rain

TUFF SHED™

>How can the wind with so many around me
>I feel lost in the city
>
>>—*Yes*, Anderson, Squire, Bruford

Delirious Rocky Mountains
He soon wood by a Tuff Shed™
Like ones he saw in front of Lowe's
Or Home Depot with window boxes

And wood shutters he would buy two
To fabricate a double-wide
Tuff Shed™ insulated against pain
For the city he had grown to dread

Constructed where a clear creek flows
Colorado's spring aspen spangle
Magpies and hummingbirds flying
Silvery black ruby red sparklers

He would need neither lock nor key
Although mountain woods be rough
On the mountain side he'd grunt
Chopping firewood and chasing foxes

Scheming for dignity in snow
He would tread softly on the land
Until friends would hike to the hut
Spring thaw to the smiling deceased

Snuggling in the double-wide Tuff Shed™
As dignified an abyss as
One can possibly hide in cavernous
Deep craggy mountainous retreats

THE LAST QUESTION

"How can the net amount of *entropy* of the universe be massively decreased?"

—Isaac Asimov

These final questions I ask
With "Insufficient data for meaningful answer"
Dysentropy being the second law's
Equal and opposite reaction

Such that dark matter's light
Anti-light is not black light's
Shadows of shadows of 4-23-73
Massive neutrinos' flight

Bubble cosmoses collisions
Informing the brane of an
Axis of evil's holes in socks
Inflationary in the TOEs

A hundred billion stars in
A hundred billion galaxies in
A hundred billion neurons in
Six billion human minds

Asking why
Diagonalized rationals
Yield transfinite transcendentals
And diagonalized transcendentals
Yield what?

Nature—a creation
From Kant's categories
Projected are not
The last questions asked in
Universes of doubt

SHANNON'S LAW

> The name of the healthy twin, hyperuniverse I, is Nommo. The name of the sick twin, hyperuniverse II, is Yurugu. These Names are known to the Dogon people of western Sudan in Africa.
>
> —Horselover Fat

Exquisite communications channels
$C = W * Log_2 (1 + S/N)$
Or information in bits
Equals bandwidth times
The natural logarithm of
One plus the signal
To noise ratio
Means that the bit content
Of a Universe is its
Fourier signature 10^{128} cps
Or E8 rotated through
Hamiltonian vector space
Bits to analog encoded
Within messages from nobody
About ethereal nothings encrypted
Texted without texture
Twittered without Klee's
"Twittering Machine"
Tweeted without Tweety Bird
Blogged without the bologna
Fragile "In and Around the Lake"

Messages to and for
Nothing from nobody
A grand façade
About nothing
Transmitted between
Universes as radiostations
Radio Free Albermuth
Itself a communications channel
About nothing
And when the $S/N = 1$
You get a one bit singularity
And when $S/N = 20$ you get
The entropy of cosmoses
And when you get $S/N = 0$
The noise becomes infinite
And that's the ultimate static
Of $1/\infty$—DEATH is
Nommo/Yuguru = 0
And the immortality
Of sanity is
Nommo/Yuguru = 1
Death is only a
A noisy state of affairs
In an Information universe
The eternal message from nobody
About nothing in particular
Static bits of no information
Blu-Ray®
Dolby-Surround®
Hi-Def®
Plagiarized
Ersatz
Big™ time
TM™
Time^(Pat. Pend.)

O LIGHT!

The poetically wise
Wizened preference to
Inhabit the shadows
Paranoia's "I don't want to be happy"
"I want to be sad"
"Sunshine sunshine"
Dun na dun na na
Sunshine
Sunshine
So the cartoon sez
Onna DuMont tv network
Circa 1953
Haters of the light
Launching milk bottles
Of light
O! Light!
Lighting up the Nazi
Haters like X-ray skeletons
Dying Goethe's plight
Power of milk
Young Werther's flight
Florescently bright
"Bring me a light"
Until the poets plead "no"
To writing on light
So I shut down
The computer
And walk with Molly Moo Cow
Into "The Cartoons Time Forgot"

OLD MAN SHOPPING

He's walking through the mall parking lot
Thinking he might be purchasing IT™
The last thing he'd buy in this life
At the mall grand mal
Petit mal seizures
Pall mall
Willy-nilly
Between the stalls
White parking lines
Twixt the stores
Too close to re-park
Re-drive
Sun glinting on his
Left eye
Destination right
Walking diagonally
Across the lots
Sub-lots with their
Parallel white lines
Dividing the slots
Into perfect spots
To pretend to want
IT™ because
IT™ is on sale

MY HVR-1 MTDNA SEQUENCE

It is proper to say we appear to be memory coils (DNA carriers capable of experience) in a computer-like thinking system which, although we have correctly recorded and stored thousands of years of experiential information, and each of us possesses somewhat different deposits from all the other life forms, there is a malfunction—a failure—of memory retrieval.

—Philip K. Dick, *VALIS*

ATTCTAATTT	AAACTATTCT	CTGTTCTTTC	ATGGGGAAGC	AGATTTGGGT
ACCACCCAAG	TATTGACTCA	CCCATCAACA	ACCGCTATGT	ATTTCGTACA
TTACTGCCAG	CCACCATAGA	TATTGTACGG	TACCATAAAT	ACTTGACCAC
CTGTAGTACA	TAAAAACCCA	ATCCACATCA	AAACCCCCTC	CCCATGCTTA
CAAGCAAGTA	CAGCAATCAA	CCtTCAAACTA	TCACACATCA	ACTGCAACTC
CAAAGCCACC	CCTCACCCAC	TAGGATACCA	ACAAACCTAC	CCACCCTTAA
CAGTACATAG	TACATAAAGC	CATTTACCGT	ACATAGCACA	TTACAGTCAA
ATCCCTTCTC	GcCCCCATGG	ATGACCCCCC	TCAGATAGGG	GTCCCTTGAC
CACCATCCTC	CGTGAAATCA	ATATCCCGCA	CAAGAGTGCT	ACTCTCCTCG
CTCCGGGCCC	ATAACACTTG	GGGGTAGCTA	AgGTGAACTG	TATCCGACAT
CTGGTTCCTA	CTTCAGGGTC			

Quote unquoth sayist the raven
Location 16001 through 16501
Cambridge Reference Sequence (CRS)
Mutation Type substitutions at

16223 C > t
16362 T > c
16482 A > g
Copying the code
Aware that I might make
Mistakes GATTACA
In my own transcriptions
Until I became a self-typing
Mutant TACA TACA
ACCA ACA TAGGA
TATTA GATTA GATTA
Tit for TAT
Genomics
& see the mutations
@ 16223/16362/16482
As broken chromosomes
From all the "boo" i
Smoked back in da' dey
B4 there was DNA
Messenger RNA and
The ACGT code
But my kids tell me
It's only "Junk DNA"
Bearing no messenger homunculus
To shoot the future y-DNA
My future mt-DNA to them
So again I check to see
If I copied the code aright
Or if nucleotide changes
Substitution mutation in the
Sequence as I copied it
From my inner cells in the
Bacchal swab to the hyplogroup
Genebase® Lab in CANADA

CAnAdA ta da to the
Email with the results
To the printer to tha
WordProcessor to the publisher
To tha to tha to tha
To the U in this poem
& as the poet says:
"U and I are born as originals
But U and I die as copies"
Miscopied hyplotypes
In DeNiAl of freedom

UNBREAKABLE CODES

Mairzy doats and dozy doats and liddle lamzy divey
A kiddley divey too, wouldn't you?

—Drake/Hoffman/Livingstone

Sequences of numbers qua number
2, 4, 6, . . .
Evens to countable infinity
0, 1, 1, 2, 3, 5, . . .
Fibonacci to sunflower
6, 28, 496, 8128, . . .
Perfects to Mersenne primes
Fascinating Möbius steps
From the Riemann known
To the Laplacian unknown

NSA employs more mathematicians
Than anyone else
Superpowers fear
Unbreakable codes
More than armed insurrections
Or the proliferation of
WMDs
Cryptographic
Platonic realms more
Real than the
Shadow plays
Of battle

Or at least
Strictly not less than
The absolute value
Of bean eaters
Who know that all
Is number

Codes beneath codes
Palimpsests
Doubly-encrypted
Paranoic analysts
Pouring over text
Wondering if the prime
Number sequence
Of words are
Al Qaeda code

The possessor of the greatest
Prime is the most powerful
Arbiter of metonymies
Substitution codes where
Everything stands for
Something else in an
Endless semiosis of
Physical objects representing

Pseudorandom number seeds
Generating Sierpinski carpets
And Menger sponges

♄♌♎♏• ♌♏♍♏♋✦♒ ♍♌♎♏•
♓♋●♓♌♏•✦•
♍♌✦♋●♌●♊♏♍♍♌♋♌✦♏♎
♓♋♋♐♌♓♍ ♋♐♋●♊✦✦
♓♌✦♌♓♐♍ ♌✧♏♌ ✦♏⊠✦
♍♌♐♎♏♌♓♐ ♓✧ ✦♒♏ ♌♌♓♌♏
♐✦♌♋♏♌ •♏♌✦♏♐♍♍
♓✧ •♌♌♎• ♋♌♏
✌● ✈♋♏♎♋ ♍♌♎♏

1,1,1,1,1,1,1,1,1,...
The first nine numbers
In N.J.A. Sloane's
Handbook of Integer Sequences
Unbreakable signs and counter-signs
In the micro psychokinesis
Of PEARS or
Princeton's Engineering Anomalies Research
And DARPA and do

THE FRONT FORTY

> The broad weedless fertilized lawns all made
> to line up flush to the sidewalk with special
> edging tools. To be honest it's all a little creepy,
> especially in high summer, when nobody's
> out and all that green just sits in the heat and
> seethes.
>
> —David Foster Wallace

I salute the Sun "Hey Ra!"
Sweating on the front forty
Glinting in the photon's reach
Radiant above the fescue
Oak leaf beaches where
The breakers wash over
The sand dunes of my cerebrum
Starting the mower's whirring
Electric nascent edger
Blower
Bagger
Limb saw
Dust mask
Yellow star
Turning into lawn
From weed patch chickweed
To golf course rough
To hayfield straw laid by
In the heather

In the gloaming
Lawnmower man
Gazing at the crab grass
Bare spots
Where nothing ever
Grows
Except the effort
Of this Looney Tune
Blade leveling boredom

TRAINING

> Cheer up, they say, the universe is ours.
> —Ruth Stone

Every blade of grass is a micro-switch
On or off in binary code
Quantum states spin-up
Spin-down monopoles of
Super-deterministic euphoria
Fine-tuned strangeness
Like training for deep-space
Space-flight's isolation
In trusting cues
In the actor's guild
Of nature's coat-tailed
Alienated magician
Presto!
Silence (check)
Blackness (check)
Com-check (check)
Nothingness (check and cross-checked)
Until solitude is absolute
No companionship sought
In the eerie quietude
Between galaxies
Training forever
For Andromeda
Or bust
Already a consummated
Hollywood cliché

SATURDAY YARD SALE

In fear of their phatic commerce
I crouch behind my drawn blinds
In utter disdain as they already trade
Used products of their own misunderstanding
Up before the cellophane dawn
Signs stapled to the autumnal trees
"Big Yard Sale Saturday"
Putting out their tables and racks
Of clothing in the oil-stained driveways
Children clamoring for more discarded
Stuff as the cars pull up and
Bored partners afraid of the
Transactions stare from the car
Behind Saturday's hangover sunglasses
And I am appalled that they
Think that their stained discards'
Negative value can be scooped
Up from moldy basement
Crawlspaces and cluttered closet
Backs of dusty garages forgotten
Implements and converted into
Positive possessions for others to ignore
Or store in their own arrays
Of commodified desperation
Displayed in their weedy yards
As fetishes to their own
Economic market failures

Over by 11:00 am's bargains
The circus moves to another
Wistfully broken neighborhood
Where violent frustration
Can capitalize upon itself
Consume its ownself
By turning sidewalks
Into shopping malls
Until in the absurdity
Of retail market exchanges
They finally sell what
They'd bought at another yard sale
At their own resale of the pre-owned
In the final cathexis of cathartic wholesale retail sale
Discount & consumerism bought & sold yin & yang
bric & brac ketch
Orgasmic fulfillment in the deal
In a suburban driveway
& shit "Sold American!"

ADDICTION

We thus become, in the absence of death as teleologic end, ourselves desiccated, deprived of some essential fluid, aridly cerebral, abstract, conceptual, little more than hallucinations of God...

—David Foster Wallace

Like tv's Detective Monk
It takes me hours deciding
Whether to put on socks
Repetitive stress disorders of
Obsessive compulsive Tang Dynasty
Astronomers *Pacing the Void*
Feints and strides into fantasy
As Newton knew tracking fluxions
And fluents into infinitesimal densities
Stretching thinly like soapbubbles
Over nothingness's *quid tertium*
Substantive sensorium's addiction
Or Leibnizian relational space
Thinking this blending flatus
So snide that hours pass like gas
In the *Infinite Jest's* boredoms
Where the "entertainment" is so
Compelling we afflictedly walk
Boogeying up and down in wheelchairs
Barefooted and conflicted but

Entertained pacing the void
Until the stars and galaxies are all
Gone to watch the entertainment
Space withdrawn to nullity and void
Absence in the glimmer
Shimmy-shimmy
Left sock
Right sock
And mow the lawn
"Co-co puff
Shimmy-Shimmy
Pow!"

NOTHING BUT NET

Hoopin' and ah hollerin'
Inspired by the cardio
Vascular benefits of hoopin'
I go out hobbled and ah stumblin'
Shootin' hoops
All five-foot seven
Of me (on a good day)
With work boots' inch-high soles
And two pairs of sweat socks
Adding stature to my game
Of one on one (myself)
Self-checking myself shootin'
Them turn-around jumpers
"Basketball Jones"
An' threes
Behind the back
Through the legs
Cross-over
Drop step
Jab step
Baseline
Shot after shot
Swish
At the buzzer!
Overcoming John Edgar's knees
At sixty-four I'mma Kobe
Phi slamma jamma

Drexler
Ah baller
"He Got game"
Practicing alone in the sun
Like Jordan for the cartoon aliens
One shot for the fate
Of the cosmos
Swish and a cracking
Net
To the rack
With ah
"Yeeeees!"
At the buzzer
From MarvAlbert

THERE BE DOZE

$$\int_{-\infty}^{x} \frac{1}{\sqrt{2\pi}}\, e^{-\frac{1}{2}t^2}\, dt$$

—Carl Friedrich Gauss

There be doze with millions of green dollars
    Holla'—but I ain't them
There be twelve year olds with perfect SATs
    Pleeze—but I ain't them either
They be people who're fulla moral virtue
    Horror—I'm not amongst 'em
There are men hung like horses
    Penile forces—eleven inch dicks
But I'm not one of them
    And there are those with youth & beauty
There are doze witty & sublime
    Famous in the city
Where I am frozen & aged in my wrinkled duty
    Shacked in the central tendencies
One standard deviation away
    Sigma squared in the propensities
Dey be doze
    Dat all dat
Daze doze
    Dat alla dat
Alla dat an' mo'
    But I ain't nunna dat

Eben doh
    Dey be doze
On der tails
    Out at three & four
Standard deviations
    I'm humanly average
And dey ain't me
    On no Normal Curve
An' I ain't dem

FOLDING THE FLAG AT ARLINGTON NATIONAL CEMETERY

> And as for the soul, what an extraordinary house it finds itself in! Who can say what it costs it, moment by moment, to accommodate itself to this residence, how much writhing and bending, folding and pleating are required of it? It was not made to live inside a thing; if it does so, under pressure of necessity, there is not a single element of its nature to which violence has not been done.
>
> —Simone Weil

Flipping the channels distractedly
A Debordian spectacle interposes itself
Again on the flatscreen rat-ta-tat
Where nine US servicemen
Tricked-out in dress hi-def unis
Dress agulettes and white gloves
Dancing around a silver-gray coffin
At Arlington National Cemetery
Going through the precisioned
Military ritual foldings rat-ta-tat
Fold & pleat relax & repeat
Muscles flexed and released
By the meticulous numbers
Creasing the Stars and Stripes
Into the Pentagon's hexaflexagons

Above the glazed body recently
Flown back from Afghanistan
Embalmed in the Mil-Spec MIL-E 1006
Arterial formaldehyde CH_2O
And glutaraldehyde $C_5H_8O_2$
All laid out in the Arlington sun
Beneath the jerky movements
Of the Honor Guards' folding
And flipping by the count
Robotic in their motions rat-ta-tat
As the nightshaded relatives
Can only bear to glance at area 60
In the steadily compressing
Triangular folding stars up
That will be presented ratcheted
And accepted before the widows
Spit and Polish rat-ta-tat
Hexaflexagon metronome
Army Reg caissons and battalions
Taps and twenty-one gun salutes
Boom boom rat-ta-tat   💣 [poem-side bomb]
By the   numb   bers with precision
Hut-two-three-four   IED-IED-IED
Love drummed into   the ground
          Crater by crater
Present Arms rat-ta-tat
With the uniform snap to returned
Valor of death's crisp salute
Twitching about your faces

OLD MAN'S SEX—A CONFESSIONAL

> And I come—spurt spurt—like bad poetry and then what?
>
> —Bret Easton Ellis

When I was a young'un it was always
Premature ejaculation
Trying to hold the little fishes back
I know they were
Tadpoles as I'd jacked off
And put them under a microscope
Little salmon leaping upstream
Shiny spawn in the exquisite
Pearled pools of masturbatory maze
Of holding back the jizsm jet
Until now that as Plato said
In his sixtieth year
"The beast has finally lifted"
Its grizzled head
Glans all flaccid
As a "postmature ejaculator"
Where imagination supersedes
Seed in utter frustration
The maturation of lust
In overlubricated love
Under testosteroned
Mightily remembered
Projectile semen launched

Toward wombs
Now barren dust
Shooting blanks
Frustrated by years of
Yearning for transcendent
Release anticlimactic reminder
Of old man sex at the end
Pitiful yet petrified
Wrinkled desiccated hairy zombie nuts
Breath stink so bad you can
Smell it with ya mouth closed
Smell it comin' round
The corner
Huffin' and puffin'
Pushin' up onya'
Panting and ah wheezing
With a throbbin' hardon

NON-RANDOMNESS

Suddenly!
Suddenly like the obituaries say
I make lists that I don't follow
Knowing what I shouldn't be doing
Living randomly hat without head
Jabberwocky "Men Without Hats"
Hiking Table Mountain in Cape Town
Table cloth off and on
Alexandria's Huntington Park
Evergreen Colorado backcountry
Reynold's Park's Hummingbird Trail
Where we scattered the cremated ashes
Of our father farther than heaven
Hiking the Appalachian Trail
In Shenandoah's National Park
("Shenandoah" means "sister of the stars"
In Cherokee—but the only
Cherokee I saw was a Jeep®)
Where the early 'Mericans walked
All the way from the lush Georgia pines
To the Stone Mountains of Maine
And the signage says that little young'en
Mary Thornton clambered up the rocks
Bringing back black bear cubs under
Each arm scrambling the blue granite
Amidst the jumbled tansies and ubiquitous
Periwinkle asters starstruck and

Mantel-bound billion year old boulders
Cracked stone and clear enough
Sky sunstrewn whetrock schist
Scintillating in the mica morning
Mists of random thoughts
Coalesced as we pass another
Backpacking tourist recognizing
Us ourselves as wearily wanting
Yesterday like the trudging
Appalachians a few years on
Oak leaves underfoot
Grist for the millstone's
"Wanwood leafmeal lie"

WATCHING TV TO RELAX

After hours of a long day
                Reading fifty thousand words
                              The literature of
Sterne's *Tristram Shandy*
Beckett's *Murphy*
Stendhal's *The Scarlet and Black*
Laxness's *The Fish Can Sing*

The retired and wistful couple
Like children "walking hand in hand"
Recline together beneath a lovingly
Knitted afghan to watch evening television

After years of "Law and Order"
"Special Victims Unit"
"Criminal Intent"
Then "CSI: NY"
"CSI: MIAMI"
Then "NCIS"
"NCIS: Los Angeles"
Then "Criminal Minds"

They've become *forensic pathologists*
Watching the nightly autopsies
Exhumations of the years old dead
The probing of lacerations
The petechiae in the conjunctiva
Gunshot residue
The Y shaped sutures

Then they became *crime scene investigators*
Gazing through the black lights for blood splatter
Semen and vaginal fluids in the rape kit
Trace DNA on the light-switch

Finally—viewing themselves victims
In the morgue's freezer
On the autopsy table
Raped and strangled

They turned to "House" to be cured
Or to be defended in the "Law"
Parts of these various "Laws and Orders"
Vicariously paranoiac and guilty
But they are always innocent
Of the mindless brutalites
Escalating metacomical violence
Calculated visual shocks
Fear inducing graphic
Makeup and Hollywood special effect
Deaths they are becoming
Every night

THE WINTER COMES TOO SOON

Somehow I've always known and
Believed they won the "Big One"
The Nazis goose-stepping
Down the black and white
Film with their ultimate
Solutions for the mud-peoples
In gas chambers where
The water in the showers
Is really good old Zyklon B
Hydrogen cyanide bubbly foamy cleanser
And fifty-five years later
A gas furnace in every house
Little gas chamber for
Each of us individually
Adjusted by the utilities
To regiment us
Welcome to the Monkey House
Retard us
Make us less than
our Aryan neighbors
Individuated gas chambers
Each of us a god damned Jew
Each a fucking deviant
Each of us queer homosexual
Each polluter of the genepool
Each of us genetically inferior
Flawed broken chromosomes

Each of us handicapped
Fuckin' crips
Each of us a nigger
Feeble-minded pea-brained coons
Each of us a medical experiment
Lab animals prepped for eugenic anesthesia
Genetic cleanliness
When winter comes in America
Decked-out in its silver-grey
Buttoned-up trenchcoat of rain and cloud
The thermostats clicking
For the first frosty thorny crystals of
A little Zyklon B for me
HCN fumigant
And a little Zyklon B for you
Mighty Nazi ruminants
As the furnace fires
Against the chill
At Dachau
At Buchenwald
At Sobibor
At Treblinka
At Auschwitz
In January dawns
Black and white geese
Lumbering through
The coal-smoked skies
Stumbling out of
Cattle cars with their
Pails of shit
Frozen in piss
And I hold my breath
'Til the hissing ends
And I see the pilot light

In the glittering smiling skulls
On the SS collars
And the black tee-shirts
In the cold morning streets
Always "The Final Solution"

U EVAH?

Realize for real 4 reel
4 evah forever
Like Cornel West sez
Paraphrasing St Augustine
Man is born betwixt piss and shit?
Or
Inter faeces et uriname nascimur
And you snapped outta it
Reanimated one day
Hyper-lucid
Meta-pellucid?
On the Metro train to Huntington Station
In the middleladay
Suddenly aware
A-where-ah
Of
The thing you have to do?
Haftta
Just haffta do
Awake and vigilant
TCB on it!
Momento mori
It's on!
"Shit on fire!"
"Fired up!"
"And ready to go!"

Me neither!

SPACE DEBRIS

For that matter
Everything changes
Is in a state of flux
$\frac{\partial M}{\partial t}$ = Matter changes in time
And in many ways Space
Qua itself is $\nabla t = \frac{dspace}{dt} \neq 0$
Or space is what time changes into
Since time itself cannot be a constant
Since everything (including time)
Is/was/will be
Time must be a change
      In something
      Unchangeable
      Like a pair of
      Doxes
      Paradoxa
      Images
      Reflections
      Holographic
      Eternities
      Outside time
      Oh my!
In a state of flux
Thus for that matter
All matter is temporal debris
Remnants of a time ·

Space continua when
It (hyper-time)
Meta-time really
Mattered back before
Hegelian conceptualization
Of the ideal of substance
In the instant before
Creation rendered the
False vacua Higgs potential
And made all this temporal
Debris space debris
    A little time dt
    A little space ds
    For everything
Reel

SUICIDE

Shirley tells me her ninety year old father
Is doing well enough to move into assisted living
And I ask her how's his appetite and she says
"He has a feeding tube and subsists on Enfamil®"
And along with him I think of suicide as a solution
And Camus'"Suicide is the only philosophical question"
And reading today that one half of all children born today
    Will live to one hundred
And I shudder that they'd better find something for them
    All to do or half of them will commit suicide
Before they're eighty in 2090
    Because without purposes
Or uses to others
    Old age becomes an excuse
To fear the unknown
    A disorder to entropy
An anomaly to neighborhoods
    An impotence to time
Infirmity to hope
    And a suicide for sure
Like eternity evaporating

OIL PAINTING

Uncompleted paint-by-number Winslow Homer
Schooner leaning into the sheets under full sail
I still remember the sweet smell of linseed oil
And the roiling grays and greens of Charles's
Roiling seas until Bertie said "But it isn't art"
And Gus allowing me to hang my smeared
"Three Bears" in his closet so "He could
See it every day before he dressed for work"

Then She painted her stiff Arctic "Penguins"
From a glossy photograph given Her by
One of Her patients for all to critique
Realism or antirealist or modernist
Or Raphael or David's Academy School
American Primitive or Grandma Moses
Or just plain old Sunday Painter
Till in one form or another we all took up the brush

So that fifty-five years after the constant redolent
Blaine Street linseed oil and turpentine basement
My house is filled with half-century old bad paintings
Already become classics of aversive scorn and
bewilderment
With no wall where a visitor or actual artist
Might glance without shame or sorrow for
These smeared "masterpieces" of conceit representing
Many others hiding in the attic or beneath the stairs

A few canvasses have escaped into the world
Gifts to relatives or friends who hang them in garages
And a few that were purchased for unknown purposes
Perhaps to provide actual examples of what art is not
And once the signature is in place I've learned leave it
Misconceived Robert Wood copies or dead pets
Studied every *faux* brushstroke and misplaced line
Perspectives for what I'd paint later in my maturity

Since I cannot draw I thought to make color my *forte*
Driven by angst and passion I'd become an
Expressionist
Slinging liquid paint and slashing bright lines into
planes
I'm Joyce Cary's Gulley Jimson in *The Horse's Mouth*
Painting to live in alzarin crimsons & cadmium yellows
With a form shaded into ultramarine violets
Until what I'd fantasized became real to me in the
canvass
Planes of color-wheeled atoms pushed into place
& as I live the *Agony and Ecstasy* of an artist
Without patrons or sycophants of the real values
Highlights from darkest darks against lightest lights
Complementary colors in Black and White coloring
books
Replacing brown gravy Rembrandts with framed
High-def flatscreen television panels as better
Because—illuminated—they move like YouTube
But I cannot escape how my old canvasses bind me

Glazed in the varnish is the complete history
Of my life like an insect trapped in amber
I cannot escape my misshapen landscapes

So I put them on the covers of my equally
Mistaken verses in these black & white colors
Of words slowly drying on the stretched yellowing
Cotton canvasses smudged forever before you

I deconstruct the dull pigments framed
Beside the 40-inch flatscreen and wonder
Why bother painting at all as it's a passé
Art form like poetry and the novel in this cybernetic
Computerized and digitized and networked
World why bother with anything except more
bandwidth
And the flatscreen tv pixilates for no reason 'cept
To remind me to compare it base 2 to the painting
Which does not and never did move
Even when I try to turn it off with the remote

EXPONENTIATION

To the nth
I have this ^{thing}
For e^{x^p} ponentiat i^{o^n}
Mathematical Up^{speak}
From Descartes' and Diophantus'
x times x = x^2
And Nicole Oresme's
x^{½} · x^{½} = x
To Cantor's alephs
And Hilbert's
"They will never remove us from these heavens above the heavens"
Mathematical hyper-spaces
Fractal Mandelbrotian decimal dimensions
Gradients for the imaginary plane's
Imaginary exponents where
Euler's Equation
$e^{i\pi}+1 = 0$
Blends transcendentals and imaginaries
Into sense
Where only
$G^{O^{D^S}}$ and $A^{N^{G^{E^{L^S}}}}$ can see that
Life is exponentiated
Squared
LIFE^{LIFE}
Is A
To tha
Iz Oh

LIKE A SHIP

> I can see by your coke my friend that
> you're from the other side
>
> —*Wooden Ships*—Crosby, Kantner, Stills

Living is like a ship
    Fore & aft
    Port to starboard
Life is a ship
    A Jefferson Airplane
    Wooden Ship
    Old creaking Square Rigger
Sheets straining to windward
    Masts leaning to
    Hull heaving to
    & climbing spume
    To westerly stars
Up & down
    Swells buoyed
    Brine to mists
Destined
    Cooperating
    Hands
A house is like a ship
    Front porch
    & back
    Hardy-Har me hardies

A star is like a ship
    Hertzsprung-Russell
    Diagrammatic drift
A galaxy is like a ship
    Hubble-Humason
    Expanding on
    An ocean of space
A cosmos is like a ship
    Singularity
    2 black energy
    Beginning to N
Destined to land
    Arrive 🚗
    After X sing 🕐 ✝🗣
    ∞ c's 👁
To home
    Is like a rebus 🌍

THE PERFECT DAY

I will not waste this day
Will not will not
I will get up and walk
Before astronomical twilight
Starlight will yet shine
Today on my face
Silver glitter on the
Mourning dove's nest
While anticipating the
Afternoon Sun
Three birds' determinism
In a cloud of ravens
Flying before consciousness
Befuddling discipline
Perusing the dysentrophic
Energies of quarks
Whirring hummingbirds
Within you/me
Dancing reels
In the perfection
Flow and eddy
Choreography from
Below quantum daylight
Noshing in the perfect
Beats to to to today
Hooray
And going with it

LOVE IS MESSY

But does not sux
& is not nasty
Because when-it-is
It is violence
Against the other
So it's messy
& sloppy as it
Entails runny diapers
Slurpy in the kissing
Droolingnesses
Bloody when in labor's
Faint inducing episiotomies
Embarrassingly nasty in
Sweet sticky sex's
Suckings and gruntings
Delivering the mess
Eros cum & lube
Glistening & wet
Onto the wrinkled sheets
Fucked up
& fucked down
& grimaced
& sweated
& screwed
& twisted
& fingered
& stroked

& loved
& squeezed
& returning it
& hard
& tight
& soft
& squishy
&
&
&
&
& O!
& release
In this
This
This exquisite
Mess

DON'T SELL ME ANYTHING ELSE

I stumble into a mall of horny shoppers
Into the thrall of cornucopious supply
Merchandise tricked out product
    Like a bruised whore
    In neon panty thongs
    Giving it up for cash
I am completed in the marketplace
All the vacuities filled solid
So I don't need anything else
    No designer slacks
    No bric-a-bracs
    No Googled facts
Don't market me for free offers
I'm a satiated *de gustibus*
Fulfilled up to my stuffed craw
    With clever by ¾ books
    With sexily seductive looks
    With jangling songs' hooks
Stop proselytizing me with the politics
Of the lovable US'es and the despicable THEM'es
From your miserable media arrayed
    In uncountable cable channels'
        Broadcast futilities
    In Sirius Radio cocker spaniels
        Barking satellites
    In sadistic movies on demandels
        Hark black light

Praise be to YOU'es to keep your Fordistic
Trucks outta my ulcerated and bereft garage
Your supermarkets overstuffed lit death
    Florescence of the consumables
    Nicked fruit for the laser scanner
    Credit carded disco discounts
And don't sell me your commercialized friendship
I'm not your friend unless I buy into IT
Spontaneity and apotheosis already obituary
    Languishing as I stutter
    Words & concepts & butter
    Imagination darkly struts
Don't sell me an apology
You're not really sorry
Because you're just sorry
    Don't sell me infinity
    Don't sell me eternity
    Don't advance me certainty
        As like a broken garbage disposal
        I can consume no more
        Need to spew it all back
Like a ticking stuffed black hole
Corpulent in having swallowed entirety
Regurgitates the digested carrion back
    Into a new universe
    Where since everything's
    Already been hocked or sold
Nothing can be bought in this new way
An apocalypse of selflessness where
There are wars for who gives most
    Hope refinanced
    Lucre of a whispered
    Desperate "See!"

For after all the World is more
Than the socially constructed
Reality of a product warrantee
    And an over burdened trash truck
    Rumbling down the street out of control
    Littering a trail of white plastic packing peanuts
        For ambling scavenging crows
        Knowing too much of the ground
        And not nearly enough of heaven
And wait!
If you order now—we'll double your order!
All you pay is shipping and handling
(Offer void where prohibited)
In a lovely gift box

FLOWCHART

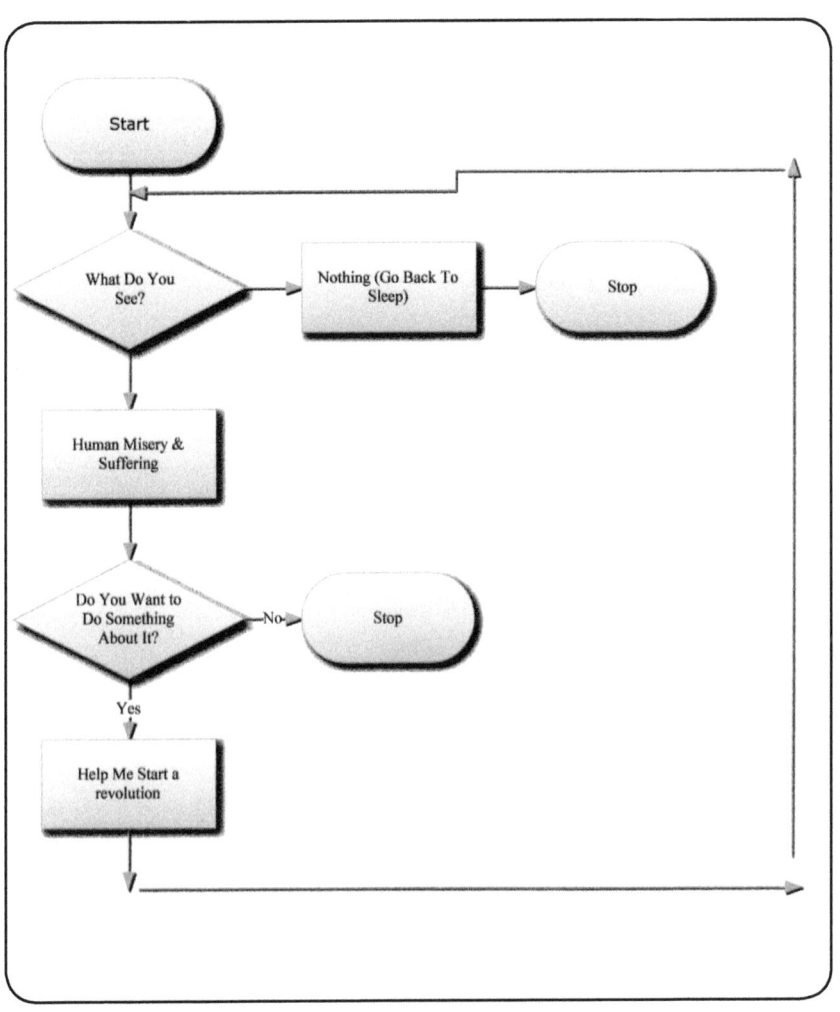

SCHIZOID RAT MAN

> Cat's foot iron claw
> Neuro-surgeons scream for more
> At paranoia's poison door
> Twenty first century schizoid man
>
> —King Crimson

Reading *Anti-Oedipus* word
    By lettered word
        Running in the "schizzes"
Flows of coding
    Counter-coded "mommy-daddy-mes"
        To the Virgin(ia) ABC Store
Alcohol Beverage Control
    Flow and counter flow
        "It's as easy as 1-2-3"
Freud's "rat man" running
    The cheese labyrinthine
        Maze to the accompanying
Aiiannaii...aaaeeeii Harpies squealing
    Schizoid wailing & keening
        Chorus for Oedipalized eternity
High-pitched astral 10^{120} cps
    Like the subway
        Jamming its brakes
Or the "Aiggh...aighhh...agiie"
    Of Alan Parson's *I Robot*
        (Chorus of every sound ever made)

The external *socius*
    Inscribed & proscribed & over-coded
        On a body without organs
That becomes and is becoming
    Everything & everybody & flows
        And counterflows of
Shit & Cum & blood & money
    In incredible historical waves of feces
        Death rattles @ "mommy-daddy-me"
The groaning tranfinite
    Changing identities in the
        Infinite disjunctions of the queue
Exteriorized in buying likker ("Lick her")
    Grid like projections
        On the surface ("Sir face")
Nursing the machinic
    Body interiorized bottle
        Robotic schizophrenic paranoic
Furtive-faced rat man

BLACK AND WHITE COLORING BOOK

Almond
Antique Brass
Apricot
Aquamarine

Asparagus
Atomic Tangerine
Banana Mania
Beaver

Bittersweet

Blizzard Blue
Blue

Bell Blue
Blue Gray
Blue Green
Blue Violet

Blush
Brick Red
Brown
Burnt Orange

Burnt Sienna
Cadet Blue
Canary
Caribbean Green

Carnation Pink
Cerise
Cerulean
Chestnut

Copper
Cornflower
Cotton Candy
Dandelion

Denim
Desert Sand
Eggplant
Electric Lime

Fern
Forest Green
Fuchsia
Fuzzy Wuzzy

Gold
Goldenrod
Granny Smith Apple
Gray

Green
Green Blue
Green Yellow
Hot Magenta

Inchworm
Indigo
Jazzberry Jam
Jungle Green

Laser Lemon
Lavender
Lemon Yellow
Macaroni and Cheese

Magenta
Magic Mint
Mahogany
Maize

Manatee   Melon   Navy Blue
Mango Tango   Midnight Blue   Neon Carrot
Maroon   Mountain Meadow   Olive Green
Marvelous   Mulberry   Orange

Orange Red   Outrageous Orange   Piggy Pink
Orange Yellow   Pacific Blue   Pine Green
Orchid   Peach   Pink Flamingo
Outer Space   Periwinkle   Pink Sherbert

Plum   Radical Red   Razzamatazz
Purple Heart   Raw Sienna   Red
Purple Mountain's   Raw Umber   Red Orange
Majesty
Purple Pizzazz   Razzle Dazzle Rose   Red Violet

Robin's Egg Blue   Screamin' Green   Shamrock
Royal Purple   Sea Green   Shocking Pink
Salmon   Sepia   Silver
Scarlet   Shadow   Sky Blue
Spring Green   Teal Blue   Tropical Rain
                                           Forest
Sunglow   Thistle   Tumbleweed
Sunset Orange   Tickle Me Pink   Turquoise Blue
Tan   Timberwolf   Unmellow Yellow

Violet   Vivid Violet   Wild Watermellon
Violet Blue   Wisteria
Violet Red   Wild Blue Yonder   Yellow
Vivid Tangerine   Wild Strawberry   Yellow Green

Yellow Orange Sun does not illuminate my racialized
world
Since Purple changed into Violet indigo

My life has been	Before and after	The Crosby Show
Barry	Michelle	And Bo Obama
Before	Now	After
A coloring book	Without	All
The colors	In the big box of	Crayolas
My life is	A Black and White	Coloring Book
Only two Crayons	One Black	One White
Inside the	On the White	Black & White
Black lines	paper	
Black	White	Black
White	Black	White
Everyday	Scarred	By hate
My Soul	Fills in the spaces	Black
White	Black	White
While	Dreaming	In Colors like
Black Kindness	White Understanding	Black White
White Black Shimmering Transcendence	Black Neon Swirl Unity Gray	White Rainbow Humanity
Color Equality	Spectra Peace	Bright Whack
Whack Bright	My B &W Colors	Transforming
On the page	Into unnamed	Yet to be seen
Colors	Hope Black	Peace White
Equality Purple	Justice Crimson	Humanity Green

FEAR OF LISTENING TO MUSIC

For months and months I have been afraid of
🎵 music for some reason or
Unreason the rhythms and the octaves
...Two, three, four...
I cannot brave the possible
$2^{(n*(n-1)/2}$ connections
 Of the neurons in my brain
Like felted hammers
On stringed reality
Itself over produced auto-tune
Chords stacked on melodies
Too harmonious
Too many tracks
Too Theolonius's
    Epistrope Round Midnight
Too Steely Dan's
    Walter Becker's *Bodhisattva*
Too Fleetwood Mac's
    Oh Well..."*I can't help about the shape I'm in/*
    I can't sing/ I ain't pretty/ And my legs are thin/
    But don't ask me what I think of you/ I might not
    Give the answers that you want me to/...Oh Well"
Dry atoms in the micro tubulin
    What the Bleep do We know?
Deaf decoupling magnetic pick-up
    Marlee Matlin's Children of a Lesser God

Amped-up and rippling down
sliding glissando up and down and back
Like the notes they mimic
Serious felted hammers
Ratcheted steel guitar strings
Oscillating thudding bass rifts
Yes
I too
Have "seen all good people turn their heads so satisfied/I'm on my way"

SIXTY-FIFTH VERNAL EQUINOX

> If you see me comin', better step aside
> A lot of men didn't and a lot of men died
> One fist of iron, the other of steel
> If the right one don't git ya, then the left one will
>
> —Tennessee Ernie Ford, *Sixteen Tons*

Now that I've traversed the space around
The sun sixty-five times—I'm no longer
The Negro "boy" I started out at the "First
Point in Aries" ♈ to be—things heard before
Meanings fixed—touched the Ram's horns
"Fin no goodies—knuckle soup" I'm shooting
Marbles more precious that "Mamie Eisenhower's
Drawers" in response meaning "No effin way!"
"Knuckles up and no hunching"
Or even
    What yo' name
    Putten in tain
    Ask me again
    I'll tell you the _____
And so perverse as even to say
    I hate to talk about ya' momma
    She's a good ole soul
    She gotta ten time pussy
    An' ah rubber ass____

Fight'en words all
>   The greatest bizness
>   In the line of bizness
>   Is to have a bidness of your own
>   If you have no business
>   Make it your bidness
>   To leave other people's business ___
Or drinkin' words
>   What's tha word?
>   Thunderbird
>   What's tha price?
>   Thirty twice
>   Who drink tha most
>   Us collerd folks
Sixty-five years of these scansions
Beneath my words—a beat
Beneath my thoughts—a beat
Beneath this Sol a ___

NAP TIME

> Mature awareness is possible only when I have digested and compensated for the biases and prejudices that are the residue of my personal history.
>
> —Sam Keen, *To a Dancing God*

When I was four
To who I try to be
Now how delusory
Hallucinatory phantasmagorical
Accumulated derivatives
Of fearful dysfunctionalities
Non-appropriable
Non-associable
Cynical mirage's
Détournement major and minor
"Oxidol soap"
"Tennessee Waltz"
"The Guiding Light"
Half heard on the radio
In 1950 between doze
And nap and my mother
Speaking "You need a nap"
Sliding into Morpheus'
Unconsciousness as
Easily as a batting an
Eye decades pass

Like *still* in
"Ode to a Grecian Urn"
Passersby in the "Psychological
Room" burning flame-men
Flamingo warriors standing
On one hinged leg stuck
In the marshes of sixty year
Old dreams until now
After my lunch I shuffle
Side to side with raised arms
Like Fred Sanford mumbling about the
Coming of "the big one Elizabeth"
A grizzled Gabby Hayes
Chewing the cud of toothless gums
To nap again like a semi-coma
This time because I really
Need to work it like an *Avatar*

I AM A WORD

> Wittgenstein, who believed that everything was words. Really. If your car would not start, it was apparently to be understood as a language problem. If you were unable to love, you were lost in language. Being constipated equaled being clogged with linguistic sediment.
>
> —David Foster Wallace

Unemployed (a word) again
The classified ads said:
> Earn thirty thousand dollars
> a year at home reading. Yes,
> you can earn money at home
> by reading. Call 201-337-6134
> today, ask for Mr. Sheldon

I did not call but I read for a living
Until it was all I did for at least eight
Ten hours a day every day every day
Of the week until I was myself a WORD
Kafkaesque Samsa nee roach but the word
I'd turned into like a hungry bug
> My bug eyes ate the words
> Like letter salad when I read
> Crunching the verbal croutons
> Nouns bacon bit adjectives
> My brain digested the words
> Elucubrated dreams writing on

Blanked pyparus hieroglyphs
In dendritic hexameter
My ears are like spiral
Cornucopia horns full of
Rhythmic fruit words
And grains thrashing kernels
I smell the words in their
Redolent dusky inks
Taste the fonts and italics
Breezing twixt my lips
Are words as is my morality
Logos/logoi and I am sometimes
Bad is a word up when I get it up
Word up Word up!
Because I am a word
Therefore I am

STELLA

Powdery light
Five inches of late January snow
Scraping sidewalk
And mystified wrens pecking
Like piano hammers
On the neglected back deck
Railings strewn
With black notes of sunflower seeds
While watching for Stella
Stealthy neighborhood kitty
Whose bass cleft symphonies are the
Scattered fluffy feathers left
When finally the snow melts

SOMEHOW OBAMA DIDN'T DO IT FOR ME

BO—AO—HNIC—Rainbow People
Before Obama—After Obama
Like the first comings BC—AD
This second coming didn't quite do it
For me at least Negro 2.0 is much like
Negro 1.0 back in the days of de facto
I think of race every single day—erday—aight
Like the weather or the seasons
Manichean onyx storms of Black
And white Escher like "Devils and Angels"
    Splibs and Spades
    Crackers and Ofays
    My brothers and
    My sistas and
    Miss Ann and
    Uncle Charlie and
    My Niggas and
    My Oppressors
So I drag my Negro self across continents like a shadow
Back to sweet Mother Africa's Ma'at and nem in Cape Town
Shaka Zulu on a Boeing 757 smokin' twenty hours and a
Black sky over Dakar crammed into a space not even
Chained slaves back in the Middle Passage would have
Cottoned to to see my blessed foremothers and nem

      Making beaded necklaces
      Batiked trinkets for the guilty
      Bourgie Black and white
      Tourists' dollars bartered
      Consciousness in the Townships
      Drumbeating in the McDonald's
      A hustle in the bustle
      Red highlights beneath the
      Khoisan's blackest innocences
Until claimed identity denied like
So much checked luggage I in
My blackness return to the US
Without even being black
A Negro 2.0 without a tribe
Or even a chief AO to honor
      Defeated I conclude
      Rainbow Nation—Rainbow World
      Nigga 3.0—version 2—release 6

GRAND PAPPY HIPPIE

Just the IS-ness.

—*Be Here Now*, Baba Ram Dass

As he got older
The more he looked like a
Jerry Garcia dumpy hippie load
And he tol' em
Truckin' half-jest
Half-serious that
All he wanted was to
Smoke some high-grade
Boo on his 75th birthday
Old hippie that he was
Cheech and Chonga
Bong or blunt didn't
Matter but the kids all
Tol' him not to do it
Cause the modern day
Sensimillia wasn't like
The Kansas ditch weed
He'd smoked back in the day
As it was 50 times as potent as
The Panama Red or the
Acapulco Gold or the
Jamaican Ganja weed mon

Yet he persisted that he
Wanted that Loco weed
Ignoring the youngens'
Admonitions that he needed
To work up on it by tweeking
Some X and other designer drugs
And shit before he could handle
The "ballroom without a parachute"
Bob Hope bud's the 420

So the old hippie smiled
High as Mr. Natural
Stepping to eternity
Foreshortened head leaning back
Truckin' foot projecting large
Stroking his white whiskers
Biding his time and
Knew he'd wait
Just a little longer
For his Oxy lollipops

www.ingramcontent.com/pod-product-compliance
Ingram Content Group UK Ltd.
Pitfield, Milton Keynes, MK11 3LW, UK
UKHW041419180426
11947UKWH00007B/224